Florence Travel Guide for Women

For Women, by Women: The Insider's Guide to the "Cradle of the Renaissance"

By Erica Stewart

© 2017 by Erica Stewart
© 2017 by ALEX-PUBLISHING

All rights reserved

Published by:

ALEX-PUBLISHING

© Copyright 2015

All rights reserved. No part of this book may be reproduced or transmitted in any form or by any means, electronically or mechanically, including photocopy, recording, or by and information storage or retrieval system, without the written permission from the publisher, except in the case of brief quotations embodied in critical articles or reviews.

Trademarks are the property of their respective holders. When used, trademarks are for the benefit of the trademark owner only.

DISCLAIMER

The information provided herein is stated to be truthful and consistent, in that any liability, in terms of inattention or otherwise, by any usage or abusage of any policies, processes, or directions contained within is the solitary and utter responsibility of the recipient reader. Under no circumstances will any legal responsibility or blame be held against the publisher for any reparation, damages, or monetary loss due to the information herein, either directly or indirectly. Respective authors hold all rights not held by publisher.

Author's Note

Florence, the birthplace of the Renaissance, literally transformed the way we saw the world for years to come. It has always been responsible for capturing the imagination of its visitors, be it with its phenomenal art, stunning natural beauty, inspired accommodations or beautiful lifestyle. Florence is perfect for anyone woman wanting to explore the best of both worlds, historic and modern, in the same tour. Its burgeoning Italian and Renaissance art collection, beautiful cathedrals and wonderful architecture are ably backed by a lively nightlife, exciting after-dark venues, an easygoing lifestyle and cosmopolitan delights. And best of all, it's completely safe for solo travelers as well!!

Florence knows that she's incredibly beautiful, but she tends to keep to herself. Her palaces look staid and dull and her architecture is certainly not showy. But as the harsh rays of the sun break away and the city is bathed in moonlight, her glowing colors make you realize just how beautiful she truly is. It becomes impossible not to fall under her spell. To explore Florence and have the time of your life, you need to arm yourself with a trusted travel companion who stands by you at every step and helps you make the right decisions at every turn.

This Florence travel guide tries to do just that with tidbits of information that let you find the right restaurants, stay in the best hotels (without breaking the bank), visit the hottest nightclubs and burn those credit cards in shopping venues that are actually worth it. This guide also acts as your personal advisor and helps you figure out what to see and what to miss (based on your preferences), explore hidden discoveries and admire the finest collection of Renaissance art the way it should be admired.

From insider tips to fun and detailed information, from attraction insights to fascinating details, from travel tips to shopping advice, everything that you need for that perfect Florence adventure can be found here.

Table of Contents

Author's Note 2
An Introduction to Florence 4
    Overview 4
    Essential Information 6
    History and Culture 7
Getting There and Around 8
    Getting There 8
    Getting Around 8
Staying in Florence 9
    Hotels for Every Budget 9
Things to See and Do 11
    Walking in the Footsteps of Michelangelo 11
    Best Neighborhoods 12
    Top Attractions 13
    After Dark 14
    Spa Guide 15
Retail Therapy 17
    Shopping Hotspots 17
    Shopping According to Need 18
    Opening Hours 19
Food and Wine 20
    Sandwich Shops 20
    Cafes 20
    Lunch 21
    Dinner 22
    Gelatos 23
    Wine Guide 24
    The Chianti Wine 24
    Best Wineries and Vineyards 24
    Osteries to Visit 25
Mark Your Calendar 26
    Top Annual Events 26

Travel Advice	27
Packing Tips	27
Insider Tips	28
**** PREVIEW OTHER BOOKS BY THIS AUTHOR****	30

"ROME FOR WOMEN: THE ULTIMATE TRAVEL GUIDE FOR WOMEN"

An Introduction to Florence

Traveling to Florence means putting up with her constant tantrums. Ignore her and you end up having an average time while in the city. She won't bare it all even if you return time and again. But pay her some attention and show her some love, and she really delights you with everything that you could possibly want in a perfect holiday. She might be small in size when compared to some of her cousins around the world, but weak she is not. Florence is busy, incredibly romantic, extremely moody and even more passionate. She's a work of art. She hasn't changed her character since the Renaissance era and each of her streets have their own stories and tales to tell. Her food and wine is so amazing that the hashtag #florentina is enough to bring you a gazillion likes, and her sense of fashion is so strong that even designers like Roberto Cavalli and Gucci decided that they would be born here.

Overview

The world-famous statue of David, made by none other than Michelangelo himself might be as iconic as the city itself, but that's not all that the City of Stone has to offer. Sure, this 17-foot marble beauty is the undisputed masterpiece, but there are other artistic wonders to admire as well. Florence usually comes across as a serious city, a city with a steely grit and a city with a soul. And this combination of strength and affection is perhaps best portrayed in the statue of David, who for all of its strength and poise has pupils that are carved in the shape of hearts.

You might believe that Florence, one of the most popular travel destinations in Italy, finds it difficult to compete with superstars such as Venice and Rome to vie for your attention, but her beauty is such she still manages to captivate you and leave you spellbound despite all those riches and adventures that other places have to offer. The city of Florence has also been termed as a UNESCO World Heritage Site, and once you descend onto those cobblestone streets, it's easy to understand why.

Florence's city center is her main attraction as it houses some of the greatest works of art in the world as well as some of the most stunning monuments, cathedrals and churches, but the surrounding countryside is equally popular for its rolling hills, lip-smacking wine and breathtaking natural beauty.

The climate is usually characterized by cold and damp winters and hot and humid summers. April to May is the best time to visit the city, as the temperature is usually pleasant and the summer crowd is still to arrive. But, the autumn season is also known to offer an extremely picturesque setting and a delightful stay.

Come to Florence, get inspired by her artwork, sample her delicious food and wine, spend your money in some of the best fashion boutiques and enjoy some quality "me time" in a destination where past and present literally mean the same thing.

Essential Information

Language: Italian

Currency Used: Euro

Telephone: +39 (Italy), 055 (Florence)

Time Zone: GMT + 1

Post Office: Via Pellicceria 3, Florence

Main Airport: Peretola Airport, Via del Termine 11, Florence. +39 055 30615

Main Taxi Companies:

- SO.CO.TA. – +39 055 4242
- CO.TA.FI. – +39 055 4390

Chemists: Open from Monday – Friday, 09.00AM to 13.00PM and 15.30PM to 20.00PM.

Emergency Contact Numbers:

- Police – 112
- Fire – 115
- Ambulance – 118

History and Culture

Any Florence travel guide can never be complete without detailing its rich history and culture. Our guide might specifically cater to our female readers, but it's still important to understand the area's history and culture, isn't it?

The history of Florence can be traced all the way back to the Etruscan times. The city was then known as Fiesole, one that dominated the entire region and was one of the most important Etruscan centers. As the Romans prepared for their war against Fiesole, they set up camp by the Arno River in the 1st century BC. This area was later called Florentia, which can roughly be translated to "destined to flower". Florence somehow managed to survive the Middle Ages as well, and soon became one of the most important cities on the planet.

Florence's growth suffered a major setback because of a dispute between the Ghibellines, those loyal to Emperor Frederick II, and the Guelfs, those loyal to the pope. This led to the Guelfs being exiled from the city, but their absence was apparently short-lived, for they took over Florence once the Emperor succumbed to his death. Despite all the political turmoil, great attention was paid to arts and architecture, and this is one of the main reasons why Florence stands like a shining architectural jewel and a stark reminder of the romantic architectural wonders of a bygone era.

Art and culture were integral to the way of life as well. The desire of its locals to educate themselves led to the birth of the first works in the vernacular language in the form of "Dolce stil novo". This later inspired countless artists such as Boccaccio, Dante and Petrarca as well. In fact, Boccaccio's documentation of the Florence plague is one of the most accurate descriptions of a tragedy that began as dissatisfaction and ended with the "Tumulto dei Ciompi" in the year 1378.

Florence saw a small period where the people took over the rule of the city. However, this was evidently short-lived as the Medici dynasty soon took over. The Medici emperor Lorenzo il Magnifico was also responsible for much of the city's wonderful Brunelleschi architecture. After his death in the year 1492, the city once again fell into turmoil, but this era of conflict still managed to see the rise of world famous artists such as Leonardo da Vinci and Michelangelo.

From the 18th century up until the very beginning of the 20th century, Florence remained famous for its literary offerings and artistic wonders. It produced some of the best works of literature created by writers such as Palazzeschi, Papini and Pratolini, all of whom were members of the literary group "Giubbe Rosse".

Getting There and Around

Florence is well-connected to the rest of Europe and is easy to get into. It has witnessed a drastic increase in tourism over the past few years, and this has led to the development of all sorts of high-tech facilities and traveler-friendly infrastructure.

Getting There

The best way to travel to Florence is by air. The Aeroporto Firenze-Peretola is the main airport of Florence and is located at a distance of 2.5 miles from the city center. The ideal way to commute from the airport is to board the shuttle bus which connects the airport to the Santa Maria Novella station and runs at intervals of 30 minutes between 06.00AM and 11.40PM. Taxi services are available as well.

Getting Around

It makes sense to leave your cars behind while traveling to Florence. And even if you're coming from a faraway destination, forget all about that car rental. As women, one of our main concerns is our security, particularly when traveling to different countries. However, when it comes to Florence, you really don't need a car for most of its major attractions are located in its historic city center, an area best explored on foot (vehicles aren't allowed to enter the city center without prior authorization either). And visiting other destinations is easy as well, for Florence boasts of a decent public transportation system that lets you get from point A to point B without much fuss.

I recommend using the taxi services while in the city, particularly if you're traveling alone. Florence taxis are white in color and can be picked up from a taxi rank or be booked on the phone. Taxi ranks can easily be found in front of the main plazas and railway stations. Some of the top taxi operators in Florence include SO.CO.TA (+39 055 4242) and CO.TA.FI (+39 055 4390).

Florence is relatively small, and this means that a woman can really have a blast while exploring its streets on a bike. There are a number of cycle tracks in the city as well, and this certainly makes things easier. Some of the top bike rental companies to hire your bikes from include Alinari (+39 055 280500), Rentway (+333 9619820), and Florence by bike (+39 055 488992).

For women who like to keep it adventurous, the Segway offers a fascinating option of getting from one place to the other. It's convenient, it's simple and it's certainly super exciting. You can book your Segways by calling +39 055 2398855.

Finally, it is very hard to resist the romantic feel of riding in an open carriage. These enchanting rides transport you to a bygone era and Florence's enchanting cobblestone streets offer the perfect backdrop to relive yesterday. You can easily pick up a carriage in Piazza San Giovanni, Piazza Duomo and Piazza della Signoria.

Staying in Florence

Florence is one of the top cities in Italy for any woman wanting to choose from a wide range of safe, secure, exciting and inviting accommodations. Florence was among the first cities in Italy to develop its hotel scene, particularly because of the efforts of local designer Michele Bonan, who has now left his mark on hotels across the country, and the hospitality division of the Ferragamo Group, Lungarno Hotels.

Hotels for Every Budget

The city has always enjoyed a great tradition of hospitality and she takes a lot of pride in introducing her female travelers to some of its best-kept secrets. There's a lot of choice across all budgets, even in the historic city center, the place where you really want to be. Better yet, the competition amongst hotels keeps rates at a low, particularly during the off season.

For Ladies Wanting to Live like Locals

If you're dreaming of staying in an area that is full of artisan workshops, real people and hidden cafes, look no further than the Oltrarano district. Some of the top accommodation options include the cute B&B Floroom 1 and the Palazzo Magnani Feroni.

Billed as one of the top bed and breakfasts in the city, **B&B Floroom 1** is a sleek address located on the banks of the Arno River, and one of the top choices for solo female travelers looking for budgeted options in the city. This four-bedroom B&B boasts of an extremely relaxed atmosphere and each of its four rooms feature wooden floors, white walls, rustic ceilings and giant photographs of Florence. The old-new combination works quite well and really makes the property stand out. Some rooms also boast of four-poster beds, and an opaque glass wall hides away the comfy bathroom that has been fitted with pewter fittings and rainforest showerheads.

The **Palazzo Magnani Feroni** is one hotel that you'd never want to leave. It makes you feel like the nobility of yesterday and transports you to a historic location that makes you forget about everything else. Each aristocratic suite boasts of beautiful high curved ceilings and heirloom furniture and the terrace views rank among the very best.

For the Budget-Conscious Woman (Medium Range)

Casa Di Barbano is a simple option that offers great value for money. It is spacious and elegant and its owners are extremely friendly. All rooms are comfortable to say the least, and when you factor in the convenient location, safe accommodations, and reasonable costs, you have everything you need to explore Florence like a pro.

Casa Nuestra is one of the hippest addresses in the city. This brand new B&B is located close to the Campo di Marti station, and is characterized by its super friendly hosts. Apart from offering picture-perfect accommodations, the owners also go out of their way to assist you in planning your itineraries, show you how to explore the city and help you uncover enchanting walking paths.

For the Lady Who Travels in Style…. (Luxury)

Palazzo Vecchietti is one of the most elegant and beautiful hotels in the city. This boutique hotel boasts of stylish rooms, easy access to Via Tornabuoni and a superior level of service. The furnishings have been tastefully appointed, and great attention has been paid to every detail. Beds are comfy and usually include quality beddings and cashmere blankets. They are the just about the perfect places to snuggle into after a long and tiring day exploring the artistic wonders around the city.

Another popular option is the **St. Regis Hotel**. It boasts of a unique ambience that is both delightful and discreet at the same time. The hotel is located on an enchanting riverside location in centro storico and its Arno views appeals to female travelers who are accustomed to the highest standards of pampering. The service is warm and welcoming, professional and casual, discreet and attentive. Everything you'd want it to be. And the rooms are just what you'd expect from a hotel like St. Regis. I would recommend the Bottega Veneta suite, a top option for fashion-conscious women.

Things to See and Do

No matter how many times you come to visit this iconic beauty, you won't be able to see it all. A bridge on the Arno River is one of the first destinations that you should visit while in Florence. It is known to offer different experiences at different times of the day, for the views, the light, and the atmosphere changes each and every time. Considered to be the birthplace of the Renaissance, Florence also boasts of some of the best art and architecture in history. No wonder it manages to draw millions of tourists year after year.

Walking in the Footsteps of Michelangelo

Very few artists have managed to leave their mark on a city the way Michelangelo has in Florence. The city is home to some of his greatest masterpieces, and one of the biggest charms of visiting the city is to retrace his steps and explore places that are linked to his memories. Embarking on the following itinerary not only lets you retrace Michelangelo's steps, but also brings you closer to some of the most important arts and monuments in Florence. Remember, the ideal way to make the most of this itinerary is to spread it over two days, so that you get enough time to marvel at the various wonders and enjoy all that it has in store for you.

Start off your explorations at the **Casa Buonarroti**. Located in the vibrant Santa Croce, Casa Buonarroti is the palace where the artist's family lived. It was built by his nephew Leonardo, and passed hands from one member of the family to another until the iconic family finally became extinct. Casa Buonarroti hosts some of the earliest works of Michelangelo such as the *Madonna della Scala* and the *Battle of the Centaurs*. The former is a tribute to sculptor Donatello while the latter has been inspired by the Garden of San Marco. Both masterpieces were created by the artist while he was in his twenties, and imagining a young boy creating such outstanding works of art is an exciting experience in itself.

The next destination is the **Church of Santo Spirito**, another place that has been intricately linked with Michelangelo during his early days. Located in the Oltrarno district, the church is considered to be one of the most beautiful Renaissance-era churches on the planet. It was also the place where Michelangelo found accommodation after his patron Lorenzo de Medici died in the year 1492. The church is famous for its inspiring wooden *Crucifix* that Michelangelo created in the year 1493.

The next step of your journey takes you to the **Bargello Museum**. Michelangelo was forced to move to Rome in the year 1494 after the city riots sent Medici into exile, and it was in Rome that he created the world famous *Bacchus*, now located in the Bargello Museum. The museum is also home to other popular artworks created by the artist such as *David/ Apollo, Brutus,* and *Tondo Pitti*.

Don't forget to add the **Accademia Gallery** into your itinerary as well. Once Michelangelo returned to Florence in the year 1501, he set about creating some of his best works of art, including the outstanding *David*, now located in the Accademia Gallery. The Accademia is also home to many of his unfinished figures and sculptures. From the *"non finito"* sculpting techniques of *St. Mathew* to the marble wonder *Prigioni*, the Accademia truly showcases some of the most the distinct features of Michelangelo's style.

Head over to the **Uffizi Art Gallery** next. Considered to be one of the most famous art galleries in the world, Uffizi features a large collection of artworks created between the 12th and 17th centuries by leading artists such as Leonardo da Vinci, Botticelli, Raffaello and Giotto. The gallery also houses the *Tondo Doni*, Michelangelo's first canvas painting and the only of its kind in Florence.

Between the years 1515 and 1534, the Medici family saw two of its members becoming popes – Clement VIII and Leo X. Michelangelo was commissioned to create the *Laurentian Library* for the *Basilica of San Lorenzo* and the *Sagrestia Nuova* for the **Medici Chapels**. Both works of art are a must see and the entire complex is also worth a visit for its artistic ingenuity.

The last Michelangelo masterpiece that you should admire during your stay in Florence is the *Pieta Bandini*. This dramatic work of art was created in the year 1550 and is now located in the **Museo dell'Opera del Duomo**. It is considered to be one of the greatest examples of the master's work and what makes it even more special is his self-portrait, a male figure flanked by Mary and Magdalene, holding the lifeless body of Christ.

Best Neighborhoods

When planning any vacation, one of the biggest concerns for women is to choose the right neighborhood. There are some areas that have traditionally been famous for being safe for women, while ensuring that they don't miss out on the very best of nightlife and cosmopolitan delights that the city has to offer. When it comes to Florence, you need to decide between three choices – staying in the historic center, staying outside of the historic center or staying in the surrounding countryside. All three areas have safe neighborhoods for women, so it ultimately boils down to personal preference. Here are a few options to choose from.

Staying Within the Historic Center

The city center always dominates a major part of your holiday for most of the historic sights and attractions are located here. The area is among the oldest parts of the city, and the ring that you see is basically the spot where those 13th century walls were built. The city center is quite small, and car free as well. This means that you can easily walk from one place to the other and not miss a car throughout your journey. Staying close to the Santa Maria Novella station puts you within a 5-minute walk from the Duomo and staying close to the Duomo pits you within a 5-minute walk from Ponte Vecchio and Palazzo Vecchio. The ideal way to choose an area is to look for accommodations close to the sites you really like. Since most of the major sites are quite close to each other, I suggest staying between **Piazza Santa Croce, Piazza San Marco, Piazza Santa Maria Novella and Pont Vecchio**. This area is among the busiest areas in the city and is always full of tourists all through the day and in the evenings as well. The second option is to look for accommodations in the Oltrarno neighborhood, but that only works if you're leaning towards local experiences, unique furniture galleries and the Pitti Palace.

Staying Outside the Historic Center

With most of the restaurants, cafes, sights and attractions located within the historic center, you would argue if it makes sense to stay outside the center. However, many female travelers visiting Florence end up booking accommodations outside its historic center for all sorts of reasons. The biggest advantage of staying outside the city center is that it is friendlier on the wallet. Moreover, anyone wanting to stay in a residential area to explore the local way of life needs to step outside the touristic city center. A few areas that aren't really far from the main sights of the city include **Via Bolognese, Fortezza da Basso, Poggio Imperiale and Piazza Beccaria**.

Staying in the Surrounding Countryside

If you're thinking of keeping Florence as a base for exploring Tuscany, you might want to head over to the surrounding hills. Apart from letting you get up close and personal to nature, it also lets you enjoy all sorts of amenities such as gardens, outdoor areas and swimming pools in your accommodations without forcing you to pay through the roof. Having your own rental car is a must while staying in the outskirts, but it's perfect for exploring Tuscany to its fullest.

Safety Concerns

Florence is an extremely safe city to visit. Most major cities have a few "shady" neighborhoods that are best avoided by women, but there really isn't any such issue in Florence. Sure, it has a few rundown streets that are littered by graffiti, but considering how small the city really is and the number of people it attracts each year, you're likely to find all of Florence safe. It's not like Florence doesn't suffer from crime, but in most cases, the crime is usually petty, and the main thing you need to be concerned about is pickpockets or people trying to take you for a ride.

Top Attractions

Looking for some of the top things to do while in Florence? From exciting museums to beautiful churches, from historic superstars to some much-needed retail therapy, here are just some of the exciting options you simply cannot ignore.

The Superstars

First up, let's talk about some of the attractions that you simply cannot miss out on while visiting Florence. Each of these ancient wonders promises an exquisite journey, an unforgettable experience and some of the best artworks in the city.

Palazzo Vecchio is located close to the Galleria delgi Uffizi and is considered to be the best museum in the city. Its gallery is home to a number of breathtaking sculptures, including a fake of the statue of David. The museum inside the museum is known to be equally exhilarating. Don't forget to visit the map room and make sure that you climb the tower to enjoy some of the best views that Florence has to offer.

The Duomo dominates the city's skyline and is one of the first attractions that you're introduced to the moment you set foot in Florence. It might attract huge crowds and come across as "touristy", but it is also known to be incredibly beautiful. You need to climb 463 stairs to get to the very top, and the climb isn't easy as well. That said, climbing to the top of the dome is totally worth it because it lets you see the entire city and feels incredibly romantic. This is also the place where you're likely to be pestered by gypsies and peddlers, so it would make sense to hold onto your belongings.

The **Ponte Vecchio** is another attraction that you simply have to experience. It is the oldest bridge in the city and is covered with artisan jewelry shops that really make you want to splurge. The place is great to enjoy an evening walk as well, particular once the bridge gets lit up after sundown.

Finally, pay your tributes to Michelangelo and Galileo at the **Santa Croce**. This humongous church also has a tomb that is dedicated to Dante. I recommend visiting the leather school inside the church, for this is where you can buy top-notch leather goods in the city.

Museums

Like most cities in Italy, Florence is big on its history. It is home to all sorts of unique museums which offer a peek into the history of Florence and all those ancient cultures as well.

The **Galleria delgi Uffizi** should always be your first stop. It is home to a fascinating collection of artwork and it doesn't restrict itself to works from Florence either.

I would also recommend a trip to the **Pitti Palace** and the **Boboli Gardens**. The place used to be the traditional home of the Medici family and the Gardens are one among the best examples of Renaissance-era gardens. The Pitti Palace is equally exciting, with its fascinating artwork and exotic architecture. You can still find a number of frescoes that used to adorn the rooms when the Medici family lived here. Don't forget to carry some water and wear walking shoes for this particular expedition.

Another popular museum worth exploring is the **La Galleria Dell'Accademia**. Sure, the museum takes some effort to getting to, but it really is worth all that effort. After all, the La Galleria Dell'Accademia is home to Michelangelo's David statue, the most popular artwork in the city.

After Dark

Florence might be most popular for its spectacular art, architecture and shopping, but once the sun goes down, its nightlife becomes the star attraction. Whether you're traveling to the city in a group or as a solo traveler, you will never find Florence wanting in terms of safe and exotic nightlife destinations and world-class nightclubs. What makes Florence so special for women excited about nightlife and after dark activities is that it is extremely safe and compact. This makes club hopping easy, and if you're living within the historic center, you don't even need a car to get from one place to the other.

You would want to think about starting with a nightclub like Moyo. It's the perfect place to start drinking, and is located in the Santa Croce area, the place you'd want to spend the night in. It is also located close to some of the more popular and expensive nightclubs in the city as well, places that are best experienced around midnight. And if you're in the mood for some dancing, search for nightclubs like Space, dance clubs that always have something special to offer.

If you're searching for a destination that serves fancy cocktails, one of the hottest nightclubs to visit is **Moyo**. They really have some of the top *apertivos* in the city, and most of the drinks are affordably priced as well. The nightclub is popular among the young and old alike, and it is always best to arrive a bit early so that you can feast on some of that mouthwatering food as well.

Yab is another hot destination for women wanting to show off their fancy blazers or designer heels. Located close the historic center, it is considered to be one of the most glamorous clubs in Florence. This ultra-chic nightclub attracts a stylish clientele and boasts of an upscale atmosphere that blows your mind away with electronic, pop and hip-hop music.

Our biggest issue with the **Flo' Lounge Bar** is that it's open for just 9 months each year. Considered to be one of the most exclusive destinations in the city, it is the perfect place for any woman wanting to enjoy a classy night out. Remember, if you're planning to spend your entire night here, it makes sense to come early. Entry can be an issue later in the evening and the buffet is totally worth that extra attention.

If you plan to wear your finest dresses for the night, **YAB** is the place to be. YAB is very strict on its dress code, and this is one of the main reasons that it boasts of an extremely exclusive clientele as well. They also have a constant barrage of exciting events, so check out their website while planning your Florence itinerary.

For those interested in club music, **Tenax** is as perfect as it gets. It is located very close to the city center and most major nightclubs are within walking distance as well. The biggest advantage that Tenax enjoys is its superior quality of music, energetic crowd and world-class DJs.

Finally, women wanting to dance the night away have to visit **Space Electronic Discoteca**. There is always more than enough room for anyone looking to have a blast while dancing, and they also have some fantastic deals on certain nights, including a ladies night as well. I would recommend you to arrive as late as possible, for that's when the real party starts.

Spa Guide

Transport yourself into an opulent world of skin care and relaxation to drain out all the damaging effects of all that drinking on your skin. Florence is home to a number of luxurious spas, with many offering signature therapies and massages that are sure to feature among your fave spa experiences ever.

Soulspace opened in the year 2007 and hasn't looked back ever since. It features muted tones and relaxing lighting together with a Turkish hamam, indoor swimming pools and six treatment rooms. Guests can also choose to relax in the garden or lounge area where melodious music and delicate perfumes delight the senses in between sessions. I recommend the Aromasoul Arabian Day Spa signature treatment. This treatment is best enjoyed as a whole-day experience which involves Turkish baths to freshen your body, eye firming treatments for revitalizing your tired and droopy eyes, fruit extracts to plump up those lips, a ritual scrub that combines the very best of Mediterranean, Indian and Oriental traditions, and an Arabian massage.

Gabrio Staff can prove to be the ideal place for blissful pampering and relaxation. It is perfect for women who settle for nothing but the very best and is famous for its innovative hair care treatments where guests have exclusive access to stylists for the entire duration of their treatment. Most salons usually tend to take you to a sink where they wash your hair, but Gabrio Staff manages to make something as basic as hair washing a ritual in itself. Each guest is wrapped in a comfy bathrobe and invited to enjoy the chaise lounge. A special therapist offers the "senses massage" which is believed to help in stimulating blood circulation and preparing your mind for the upcoming relaxation. Treatments offered by the spa range from basic hair spas and beauty masques to exotic "silk treatments". I recommend the "4-Hands Hair Spa", a massage that involves using two masseuses at the same time and also includes an exfoliating massage.

The **Body Care Benessere Day Spa** is located very close to all those magical plazas, attractions and churches which means that you can always hop over when you're in need of some much-needed R&R. Spread over 2000 sq. ft., the spa boasts of 22 treatment rooms and offers guests an extremely exclusive environment for completely personalized services and treatments. The spa is a place where you get to relax your mind and body and also make the most of exciting amenities such as Turkish baths, Jacuzzis, swimming pools, multi-sensory showers and sauna. Whether it's a body massage or weight loss, whether it's an anti-aging treatment or a pedicure, the Body Care Benessere Day Spa is where you need to be.

The **Spa at Four Seasons Hotel Firenze** is located in the 11-acre private garden owned by Four Seasons Hotel Firenze. The main building boasts of polished oak flooring, contemporary mosaics and breathtaking floor-to-ceiling windows and the spa also features a relaxing cream and black interior, an exciting collection of natural products and perfectly chosen artworks. The spa is home to 9 treatment rooms, with the VIP couple's suite being the biggest highlight. It boasts of a fireplace in the lounge area, corniced ceilings, free standing bath area and a private garden to ensure absolute discretion. I recommend the Sense of Well-Being treatment, three hours of surreal pampering that takes place in this inviting suite and includes things like a pureness facial, rose water toning treatment, exfoliating scrubs and foot soaks.

Retail Therapy

Florence is home to all types of shopping delights, and there's something for all kinds of tastes here. Exploring the very best of Italian fashion is something that no woman can miss out on. It might not be as outrageous and fascinating as the shopping scene in Milan or Rome, but it's still worth a look. Moreover, there are many unique shopping adventures to be had as well.

Shopping Hotspots

Luisa Via Roma's online store has been a darling for shopaholics over the years. Ever since its launch in the year 2000, it was one of the go-to sites for women searching for all kinds of slick deals on all sorts of products and brands, right from Yohji Yamamoto to Armani. Its online website that attracts more than 30 million unique visitors each year isn't any secret, but its local store might just be one of those hidden shopping secrets of Florence. The 4-decade-old store is one of the most enticing and seductive looking stores in the Duomo area, and is particularly famous for its jaw-dropping displays. It houses all kinds of brands such as Delfina Delettrez and Jimmy Choo and close to 80% of the labels found here belong Italian designers.

Mercato Centrale is another popular shopping destination in Florence. This humongous food market is the place to be if you're searching for some authentic food and delicious smells or are simply looking to explore the local way of life.

Located in those beautiful hills of Tuscany, this is an experience unlike any other. **The Mall** isn't your average shopping mall. Much like the one in Marbella (Spain), this hidden retreat is as close to the Shangri-La of shopping as it gets. It boasts of a scintillating collection of designers and brands and is the place to be for anyone looking for dreamy labels and some of the very best fashion on the planet. The prices might be nothing short of exorbitant, but when you're dealing with brands like Armani, Ferragamo, Stella McCarthy, Fendi, Lanvin, Alexander McQueen, Burberry and Saint Laurent, prices do seem to take a backseat. To make things even better, you can expect discounts between 30% to 50% on all major brands found here.

The **San Lorenzo Market** is connected to the Mercato Centrale and is also located in close proximity to the Duomo. It is also home to the world famous Florence leather jacket. Remember, it is okay for the stall owner to take you to another store that lines the market because most stalls are just used to display the items. And even though those prices may look expensive, there's always room to negotiate.

The **Salvatore Ferragamo Flagship & Museum** is to Florence what Fifth Avenue is to NYC. It is one of those destinations where every inch is covered with some dream designer or the other. Things like Prada, Fendi, Roberto Cavalli and Fendi feel so "every day" in this area, and if you're searching for flagship stores of some of the greatest Italian brands, this is the place to be. The obvious highlight is the Salvatore Ferragamo store. Located in a humongous five-story castle, the flagship is a reminder of just why the brand is so famous all over the world. Its frescoed ceilings and fascinating architecture are noteworthy, but they really pale out in front of that dazzling collection of shoes, clothes and bags. There's an entire room which is dedicated to limited edition re-issues as well!

Raspini has often been termed as the shoe which launched an entirely new era in footwear. Considered to be one of the most popular luxury retailers of Italy, Raspini began its journey as a small shoe store in the year 1948. Today, it is a multi-brand department store which houses brands like Miu Miu, Prada and

Dolce & Gabbana, and is among the most famous shopping destinations in Italy. Beautiful aesthetics and on-point products are two of the main reasons why the brand is so famous.

Who would have imagined Guccio Gucci to become one of the greatest fashion labels on the planet in the year 1921, when he opened a tiny leather goods store in Florence! Today, Gucci boasts of more than 400 stores around the world, and is so unique in its collection of products, that it could easily boast of an entire museum of its own products. And the **Guccio Museum and Icon store** is exactly that! It not only hosts vintage photos and a great collection of regular Gucci products, but also features things that you never knew about – items like wallpapers, picnic baskets, surfboards and snorkels. The place is also home to the Icon store, home to some of the most limited-edition Gucci scarves, accessories and bags which are exclusive to the Florence address.

Most people wouldn't expect to find a place like **Bjork** in Florence. The store is just about everything renaissance-era fashion stood for, and is one of those concept stores which really bowls you over. Bjork is also home to some of the coolest products in Florence and items you wouldn't anywhere else in the city, things like LRNCE drawstring bags, Kinfolk magazines and Won Hundred clothes.

Shopping According to Need

Florence is home to all sorts of shopping opportunities. Any woman simply cannot fathom the idea of not reserving an entire day for shopping (even if it's just window shopping), for the breathtaking array of brands found here can be seen in very few cities around the world. Here's a selection of shopping areas to choose from according to your need.

Shopping for Italian Fashion

If you're searching for some of the hottest fashion in Italy while in Florence, simply head over to the Via Tornabuoni. The area is home to one of the most romantic palaces of Florence since the 14th century and is now home to many of the city's luxury shops, upscale jewelry stores and designer boutiques. Shopping in Via Tornabuoni might be way out of line for most people due to the exorbitant prices, but it is always fun to window shop and check out brands like Ferragamo, Gucci, Bulgari, Pucci and Prada. For women interested in boutique stores, the Via della Vigna Nuova, located right off Via Tornabuoni, is just about perfect. It is home to brands like Monteblanc, Etro and Lacoste. Other popular areas to search for Italian fashion include Visa Roma and Via del Parione.

Shopping for Antiques and Collectables

Women searching for antiques need to head over to Via de Fossi, a street located close to the Santa Maria Novella. Another exciting option is Via Maggio, located close to the Pitti Palace. Both destinations are famous for their antique stores which are home to an exotic collection of arts and antiques.

Casual, Trendy Shopping

Smart and chic women will simply fall in love with areas like Via dei Cerratani, Via dei Banchi and Via dei Calzaiuoli. They are home to a number of popular labels like Furla, Zara, Coin, H&M, Rinascente, Carpisa and the Disney Store.

Leather Shopping

They say that you simply cannot leave Florence without purchasing a few leather products. For items such as wallets, bags, jackets or belts, head over to the San Lorenzo Market, the mecca for all leather goods. There are a number of stores to choose from and it's possible to drive a bargain as well.

Shopping for Gold Jewelry

Those looking for gold jewelry need to visit Ponte Vecchio. It became popular because of its sparkling windows and gorgeous displays, and is home to some of the most popular jewelry stores in Italy. Apart from branded ware, you can also find all sorts of unique bracelets, necklaces, earrings and rings here.

Shopping for Food and Wine

If you're thinking about carrying exotic food products back home or are planning to cook while in Florence, simply visit the Sant'Ambrogio Market or the San Lorenzo Market for all your food and wine shopping. Both markets are home to some of the tastiest and freshest produce, and it is possible to find just about everything here. Cantinetta de Verrazzano is where you'd want to be for delicious biscuits and pastries, while Procacci is the hottest destination for out-of-the-world truffle sandwiches.

Opening Hours

Shopping in the main areas is never a problem because most of the major stores have a full working day. However, if you're more into artisan or boutique stores, you might want to stay away from shopping between 12.30 PM and 03.30 PM, as many of the smaller stores close down for lunch. It always makes sense to head out for shopping around 03.00 PM since most stores stay open till at least 07.30 PM, giving you ample time to shop. Some stores also stay closed on Sundays, but this is usually not an issue with the larger stores or stores located in major shopping neighborhoods. However, when it comes to areas like Santa Croce or Oltrarno, you can expect most stores to stay closed on Sundays.

Food and Wine

The Tuscan cuisine is famous for its use of local, fresh and simple ingredients. From world class gelatos to Michelin-starred restaurants, the city certainly has its fair share of dining wonders, but in a city where simple T-bone steaks that are cooked using chestnut wood and served with a pinch of salt and pepper and some olive oil resemble works of art, you would expect a burst of flavor and tantalizing feelings with every bite. While most places can offer that fresh and clean taste, some restaurants are known for tingling your taste buds unlike any other.

Sandwich Shops

There isn't any shortage of restaurants and cafes to choose from while in Florence, but you simply must dig into the local *panini* while visiting the city. Good sandwich shops can be found all over Florence, irrespective of whether you're in the outskirts of town or in the city center. And remember, if you can't make up your mind, just say "*Il tuo preferito*", which is same as asking for the house favorite.

I due Fratellini may be small in size, but it truly packs a punch. It is located close to the Piazza Repubblica and is home to some of the most mouthwatering *panini* that Florence has to offer. Its proximity to the main shopping areas in the city also makes this the ideal place to grab a bite in between all that shopping.

They say that to live like the locals, you need to start eating like the locals. One of the best places that offers some local fare is **All'Antico Vinaio**. The *paninis* served here boast of using the best ingredients, many of which are homegrown or baked daily.

The **Oil Shoppe** is another popular *panini* joint the city. It is very famous among the student population and the waiters here can speak perfect English. It does look a bit sophisticated, but don't let those looks deceive you. It still serves some of the best and value-for-money sandwiches in the city.

'INO is your go-to panini destination in town. Considered to be one of the jewels of Florence, this Alessandro Frasscia wonder is responsible for using the best and freshest ingredients in each of its dishes. From Sicilian cherry tomatoes to specially ordered pane toscano and ciabatte, expect 'INO to pay a great deal of attention to each detail. Look out for the specials of the day which are written on the chalkboard and blindly order what feels the best.

Cafes

The Coffee Culture: Forence may not have given birth to coffee, but it certainly gave birth to the guardians of the coffee culture, temples that the modern world now knows as cafes. What makes the cafes in Florence so unique is that Italy has an entirely unique way of drinking coffee, something that cannot be seen anywhere else on the planet. There are strict rules that need to be followed, for not following them either brands you as a tourist or gets you ridiculed. In order to follow the rich legacy left by some of the best coffee drinkers that the world has ever seen, you need to follow these rules.

1. Sitting down for coffee is four times as expensive as taking it at the bar.
2. Never drink cappuccinos after midday unless you get up late or it's exceptionally cold outside.
3. Never drink cappuccinos after a meal, unless it's your breakfast.
4. Always have coffee after your meals, never with them.
5. Latte means milk. What the rest of the world calls *latte* is known as latte macchiato and it's usually preferred by kids and pregnant women.

6. Never drink cappuccinos with savory dishes.

Best Cafes in Florence

Now that you're aware of the coffee culture in Florence, it's time to introduce you to some of the city's hottest cafes. Strict as these rules seem to be, following them in a popular café instantly makes the locals open up to you and presents an exciting opportunity to get to know them better.

Scudieri is located near Piazza di San Giovanni and is known to serve espressos that feature earthy flavors and a strong finish. The glasses used to serve the coffee are extremely beautiful as well. The atmosphere of this café is another major strongpoint. Long pastry cabinets taunt you to forget all about controlled eating while the marble bar which is topped with some silver coffee adds to the appeal. The service is also known to be extremely friendly, and a tad on the slower side, which is just the way you'd like it to be in a café.

Caffe Donnini is located close to Piazza della Repubblica and is home to a medium-to-full-bodied espresso which features a strong finish and a dark roast flavor. The coffee doesn't have as much cream, but it still has an excellent taste. Apart from serving good coffee, Caffe Donnini also serves up some of the best pastries in the city. The feels is more like a bar with all those rich colors, the gorgeous chandelier and beautiful decorations. There are plenty of tables so finding place should never be an issue, even during those peak hours.

Caffe Gilli is located in Via Roma and has a coffee that simply doesn't have enough foam and a short finish. The coffee served here is quite weak, so the café may not be an option for lovers of strong coffee. But since Caffe Gilli is located in the center of one of the most popular shopping streets in the city, you might just come to grab a bite or two. The interior is elegant and beautiful, and it literally resembles a traditional British tea room.

Oblate, located in Via dell'Oriuolo, is famous as a café that has an awesome view. Considered to be a popular place to meet up in Florence, Oblate has finally come to terms with its superstar image and now offers its guests a vast and varied list of programs that range from themed happy hours and brunch to special concerts. The prices are dirt cheap for a café of such appeal, and the atmosphere is always groovy and trendy, irrespective of the time you choose to visit. Although, you'd want to note that Oblate is closed on Sundays.

Todo Modo is a theater-cum-café-cum-bookshop that is spread over 180 sq. m. and is home to a wine bar, more than 15000 titles and some of the very best coffee in the city. The free WiFi makes social media buffs and travelers haunt the place and the lure of books is simply too much for bookworms to resist. Todo Modo has a Scandinavian design and is quite well loved by the locals. A popular place to go to any day of the week, except when it's closed on Mondays.

Lunch

La Prosciutteria is one of the best places that you can go to for lunch, particularly if you long for an assortment of meats and cheese. Order for the big board, some house wine and a sandwich. The big board contains three or four different types of cheese, four to five varieties of ham, grapes and melons. The meal is quite delicious and extremely economical, particularly if you're traveling in a group. The cheese is absolutely fantastic as well.

Trattoria Sostanza is another popular lunch destination in town. It is a huge favorite among the locals, and for good reason. The place dates all the way back to 1869 which makes it older than Italy itself! It is brimming with stories and is steeped with tradition, and the quality of food here has been consistent for decades. If you're searching for some authentic wood-burning stove cooking, this is the place to be. Order for the humongous bistecca alla fiorentina and the artichoke tart while at the restaurant.

I' Pizzacchiere is famous for serving some of the most amazing pizzas in the city. The friendly service is a huge plus, the restaurant uses nothing but fresh ingredients and the crusts are done perfectly as well. At just €8.5 for a regular pizza, you'll be filled to the brim as well. The mixed salad on pizza crusts is one of the top dishes here.

Trattoria Mario might be jam packed and super noisy, but you won't mind all that commotion and waiting once you get a whiff of its dishes. The restaurant may be extremely compact with tables being located inches from each other, but it never was big on presentation. What the restaurant does boast of is offering dishes that will simply blow you away. Order for the bistecca alla fiorentina while at Mario's.

Lastly, **Rose** is local favorite among women is another lunch destination to try out while in Florence. The place is small and cozy and it gives I'Pizzacchiere a real run for its money in terms of its quality of pizzas. Other dishes worth trying include omelets, salads, burgers, enchiladas and stuffed pitas. Complete the perfect meal with desserts like fresh fruit salad, strudel with honey and fresh muffins.

Dinner

Cibreo is your go-to destination if you're searching for some traditional Tuscan cuisine while in Florence. The restaurant is where you get to meet many of the local musicians, intellectuals and writers, and notable personalities like Woody Allen have also been known to come here. The restaurant uses the freshest produce from the Sant'Ambrogio market and tries to create a work of art in each and every dish. The homemade cheesecakes and chocolate cakes are some of the top highlights of Cibreo and the roasted pigeon with fruit mustard is equally delicious.

Alle Murate is a major Italian joint that acts as a restaurant as well as a museum. Located in the historic Palazzo della Arte dei Giudici e Notai, the frescoes found here include some of the first depictions of Boccaccio and Dante. Traditional dishes such as T-bone steaks and Pappardelle are the biggest dining highlights, while the ancient Roman foundations that can be seen in the basement keep history buffs happy and satisfied. Apart from authentic delights, the restaurant also serves a number of creative dishes such as savoy cabbage with capers and stone bass fillets with red beetroot. The wine menu features smaller producers as well as French and Italian greats. Women looking for an incredibly romantic atmosphere are sure to fall in love with the restaurant.

Enoteca Pinchiorri is a marriage between Sommelier Georgio Pinchiorri and Head Chef Annie Feold that serves up a delightful French/ Italian cuisine. This beautiful fusion initially started at the National Wine Cellar where Annie created light dishes to complement the coveted wine collection, and ended up becoming a complex three-star Michelin restaurant that serves some of the finest wine and the tastiest of dishes in all of Italy. Apart from its show-stopping dishes, the restaurant also presents an incredible character with its beautiful mosaics, antique furniture, pink marble chimneys and parquet floors.

Ora D'Aria is a popular Tuscan restaurant that was once located in a Renaissance-era woman's prison. Today, it has moved to a centralized location behind the Uffizi, but still retains some of the authentic feels in its décor. Head Chef Marco Stabile presents a white and gray décor façade and makes up for the minimalist décor by adding Galleria Bagnai artworks. The Fish themed and a Tuscan themed tasting menus always offer the best dining experiences. The restaurant also offers discrete dining arrangements for up to four people in its cellar.

Gelatos

Florence is famous for being a gelato-crazy city, and there are many gelato shops located all over, with most offering some really good gelato. However, visiting one of the following gelaterias should always present the best gelato experience in Florence.

Gelateria La Carraia is famous as the top gelateria in Florence, and for good reason. Located close to the Ponte alla Carraia, this place serves some of the softest and creamiest gelatos in the city. The tiramisu usually has the same consistency as whipped cream, and all other flavors are delicious as well. I recommend you to try out the fruit of the day which is served on the tasting cone and costs just €1.

La Strega is a gelateria that became popular for its splendid flavors and delicious gelatos. Time seems to stop here, and no one bothers you while you lick and slurp your way through that tasty ice cream. Make sure to stop by the gelateria while visiting the Altrarno area.

Carapina is another gelateria that you'd want to visit while in Florence. It is located between the Ponte Vecchio and the Uffizi Gallery and is known to be very popular among the locals. What makes Carapina a special experience is that its ice cream is made using the freshest and most seasonal fruits. It is light and creamy and you literally feel as if you're biting into the fruit when tasting those fruity flavors. The only problem? Carapina is closed for a couple of weeks in the month of August.

Gelateria Carabe is one gelateria that you're likely to dream about for months after your Florence holiday. This Sicilian gelateria serves some of the best gelatos in town and is famous for combining traditional ingredients such as Bronte pistachios and Noto almonds. One of the biggest specialties of Gelateria Carabe is the Neopolitan ricotta cake, which is specially made for Easter. The restaurant is also known for its breakfast granitas that are made using lemons, almonds and black mulberries.

Wine Guide

Have you heard of Chianti? Of course you have! Who hasn't tried out the Chianti wine!! To have wine and not try out the Chianti is something that simply cannot be fathomed by any wine lover. So if you're into the Chianti wine or are a wine lover, you simply cannot miss out on visiting the Chianti region, home of the epic Chianti wine, whenever you visit Florence. The region is located between Siena and Florence and it features some of the greatest wine-makers and vineyards on the planet. The best way to explore the Florentine wine is to embark on an exciting wine tasting tour and visit some of the hidden vineyards and wine bars located all over the countryside. This section introduces you to some of the most respected winemakers as well as some of the best wine bars in the Chianti region.

The Chianti Wine

The Chianti wine is an enigmatic wine that is made across Tuscany, but is most famous between Siena and Florence. Cosimo de' Medici III, the Duke of Tuscany, had decreed that the wine produced in this region would be the only wine that could be termed as Chianti Classico, a wine that can be easily recognized by the black rooster on its label. Chianti is a dry red wine that always feels best when paired with the right food. It is considered to be as important as virgin olive oil in the Italian cuisine, and few wines can stand up to the spicy, tarty Chianti when it is paired with some pasta al pomodoro or sliced prosciutto.

Best Wineries and Vineyards

If you really wish to understand what the Chianti wine is all about, you simply have to go and meet Roberto Bianchi at the **Val Delle Corti**. Roberto has been guiding wine gurus and wine guidebooks for years and his six-hectare vineyard produces just three wines, but all three wines are known to rank among the very best Chianti wines in Italy. Try out the elegant vino di tavola and pair it with some salami for that perfect fusion of tastes.

If you've always believed that major vineyards charge a bomb for wine tastings, think again. The **Fontodi Vineyard**, one of the most popular vineyards in the country, believes that offering guests a look into what wine making is all about is more important than selling a bottle or two. The estate is owned by winemaker Giovanni Manetti and is famous for its authentic Tuscan hospitality. It has 30 acres of olive trees and 80 hectares of vines and is considered to rank among the most beautiful estates in the country as well. You can also check out the Chianina cattle, one of the fastest disappearing cattle varieties on the planet, while at the Fontodi Vineyard.

Villa Pomona resembles those typical Tuscan estates that you often read about in novels or watch on the TV. Headed by Monica Raspi, the vineyard stretches over 4 hectares and offers the perfect mix of biodiversity and natural beauty through its fusion of olive groves, sprawling farms, vineyards and woodlands. The estate is also home to an old olive mill that has now been transformed into holiday accommodations for guests.

Osteries to Visit

A Casa Mia is one of the rarest osteries that you will ever visit while in Italy. Located in a small hillside hamlet, it features Italian home cooking at its very best. The osterie is run by two highly passionate hosts who take turns cooking and serving, and each plate is known to be so flavorful that guests are left licking their fingers and whatever tidbits that are left remaining on their plates. The antipasti dish is one of the main highlights of the restaurant. Filled with bruschetta, fresh tomatoes, grilled vegetables, panzanella and tripe salad, it is as filling as an entire meal. For the perfect experience, follow up the antipasti with some of the €10 Chianti that is served here. And always call for a reservation for the place is packed each and every night. If you're confused about what to order from that printed menu, just ask the hosts to serve the dishes of the day.

Fattoria di Corsignano

There is no shortage of opulent, luxurious fine dining restaurants in Tuscany, but finding traditional places that serve authentic cooking and are reasonably priced is another matter altogether. This is why restaurants like Fattoria di Corsignano become even more popular. The restaurant offers some of the best rustic *cucina contadino* in the region and also features a four-course wine-tasting menu for just €35. Other highlights include antipasto with smoked ham, panzanella salad, riotta and grilled zucchini bruschettas, fried bacon with prunes and barley cakes. Fattoria di Corsignano is located within an estate that is also home to a 7 acre vineyard that is responsible for producing an old-style Chianti wine that costs just €6.

Antica Macelleria Cecchini

Antica Macelleria Cecchini might be a mere butcher shop, but it looks more like a theater, a work of art even. Run by Dario Cecchini, Antica Macelleria Cecchini is famous for serving one of the best T-bone steaks in Italy, the Costata alla Fiorentina. Apart from this delightful dish, you can also ask Dario to pack the perfect picnic basket which is full of your favorite dishes, and show you the perfect picnic spot located a couple of minutes away as well. Antica Macelleria Cecchini is also famous for its hospitality and this means that the restaurant is always crowded. Expect salami, cheese and red wine to be served on each table for free, and make sure to dig into the Dario Doc, a delicious burger that sets you back by just €10.

Mark Your Calendar

Most major cities in Europe are famous for their age old traditions, steeped history and beautiful festivals. Florence is no different either. It offers some of the best festivals and events that suit all sorts of preferences and an insight into its rich cuisine and thousand-year-old culture. Here is a brief selection of some of the top festivals that you simply must experience while in Florence.

Top Annual Events

Epiphany, January

Epiphany is held on the 6th of January to celebrate the Three Kings' arrival in Bethlehem. It is popularly known as the day when Italians shower each other with gifts and also marks the arrival of La Befana, the Santa Claus of Italy. The main highlight of the festival is the Cavalcade of the Three Kings, an age-old tradition that is held in the downtown area. This unique tradition actually dates all the way back to the year 1417 and it features an enchanting parade that is full of renaissance-era costumes, stories and local folklore.

Carnebale, February

Whoever said you have to travel all the way to Rio to enjoy the carnival! Florence celebrates its very own carnival in the month of February, a festival that is just as beautiful as any other carnival around the world. It highlights different cultures residing in the city and represents local traditions through musicians, renaissance-era costumes, dancers, horseback riders and bands.

Scoppio Del Carro, April

The Explosion of the Cart, or Scoppio Del Carro, is another major event in the city. This tradition goes back 400 years and features a historic wooden wagon that is pushed around the streets of Florence by a fleet of oxen. The cart is fitted with all sorts of fireworks, the highlight being that dove-shaped rocket which always fills the sky with a plethora of colors and patterns.

Maggio Musicale Fiorentino, May

Maggio Musicale Fiorentino is a music festival that is held between the months of April to June. It attracts world-class artists and is held at various venues across the city. It makes sense to book tickets in advance, because the seats are famous for disappearing very quickly.

Florence Dance Festival, June/ July

The Florence Dance Festival is held each year at the Teatro Romano between the months of June and July. It is one of the best experiences that you can possibly enjoy in Florence, for it is held in a real Roman era amphitheater.

La Festa Delle Rificolone, September

The Festival of Paper Lanterns, or La Festa Delle Rificolone, brings the locals out onto the streets. It is held the day before the feast of the Nativity of Virgin Mary, and it usually includes Florentines walking around the streets with candle-lit paper lanterns in their hands. The main procession starts around 8 PM at the Piazza Santa Croce and goes all the way to Piazza S.S. Annunziata, and this procession is the one that you need to watch out for.

Travel Advice

Italy is one of the safest countries for women traveling alone. Most of its major cities are relatively safe, and the only crime that you need to watch out for is petty crime. Using common sense and avoiding shady areas at night or during odd hours should be more than enough to keep you safe throughout your journey. This section offers some valuable travel advice for women traveling to Italy. Whether you're looking for tips on how to pack or insider tips on how to enjoy the city to its fullest, this section has answers to all your doubts.

Packing Tips

Packing for an Italian holiday is almost like packing for any other holiday. What you carry along with you depends on your itinerary, the places you plan to visit and the things you wish to do. This "what to pack" list helps you with all those miscellaneous teeny-weeny doubts.

Be Sensible While Packing

We love to take all sorts of things with us while traveling, but the more items you carry, the more of a headache they become during your holiday. It always makes sense to be sensible while packing for a trip to Florence. Color code your outfits and mix and match pieces so that it's possible to repeat outfits without looking monotonous. Another benefit of packing light: you're going to one of the hottest fashion destinations in the world. You certainly expect to do some shopping, don't you?

What to Pack

Apart from the usual stuff, it always makes sense to ensure that you carry the following items while visiting Florence.

1. Wipes – It's impossible to get by without wipes in Florence. They can also double up as toilet paper during emergencies.
2. Sunscreen – Rather than buying some sunscreen here, always carry enough for your journey.
3. Umbrella – You'll regret not carrying one as the prices rise sky high the moment it starts raining.
4. Bikini – If you're traveling during the summers and plan to hit a beach, it makes sense to carry bikinis. You will feel odd in a monokini in Italian beaches, since women love to show off their bodies here.
5. Cover-ups – A number of attractions might turn you away if you're not properly covered up. Instead of missing out on those breathtaking masterpieces, simply carry a shoulder cover up and slip it on before entering.
6. Guidebooks – Carry paper copies of all relevant information. They're much more useful during emergencies.
7. Street Map – Always carry a street map of Florence. It can help out in the weirdest of ways and it is always handy to have one.

What Not to Pack

When it comes to things that you should avoid carrying, the list is quite simple.

1. Avoid carrying shorts unless you plan to bike or hit the beach. You'll feel extremely odd wearing them on the streets.
2. Avoid carrying the hairdryer. Most hotels in Florence (even budget ones) have them.

3. Stay away from spiked heels. Those cobblestone streets are not heel-friendly at all.
4. Leave those white sneakers at home and carry some comfy-yet-stylish walking shoes instead. Fancy sneakers or flat-heeled boots are ideal options.

Insider Tips

Florence is incredibly beautiful and will always offer a special experience. This ancient city is the best place to enjoy romantic walks, breathe in the historic atmosphere, encounter enchanting artworks and get acquainted to world famous artists such as Michelangelo and Donatello. These insider tips should go a long way in making your Florence itineraries more special, for they feature a few tips that you simply have to follow to make any Florence adventure perfect.

Take it Slow

The first thing that you need to remember is that you must always take it slow while visiting Florence. There is no point hurrying through all those exotic churches, monuments and museums and their incredible artistic wonders. The key to enjoying Florence is to ensure that you don't get overwhelmed and follow a leisurely pace as you stroll through the city. Since everything is located close by, it becomes easier to take it slow, as you're never dependent on public transport to get you from one point to the other.

Grab the Uffizi Card

The Uffizi Card gives you access to some of the top deals in the city, including a number of skip-the-line tours for popular museums. The card costs €60 and offers access to five state museums in Florence. It also lets you skip the line at the Uffizi and the Accademia, both known to host some of the top artworks in the city, including two Michelangelo masterpieces. Moreover, the card allows multiple entries into the museums, so if you're staying in Florence for a few days, it really makes sense to purchase this card.

Plan for Mondays and Be Aware of Schedules

Having a printed schedule of the timings of all major museums can come in handy while visiting Florence. Most major destinations have their own opening and closing times, and it makes sense to plan your itineraries accordingly. You can find this information on the Florence Tourism website. It also makes sense to plan your Monday itineraries as many major attractions such as the Pitti palace and the Uffizi Gallery are closed on Mondays.

Save Money on Lunch

Food is very expensive in Florence, and therefore, you would want to look at street food or snacks when it comes to lunch. If your hotel offers complimentary breakfast, it always makes sense to eat heavy in the morning and follow it with some light lunch. There are all sorts of small places that offer economical options such as the grocery chain Conad. The local *paninis* are an ideal alternative.

Buy Italian Shoes at Great Discounts

Florence is home to a number of discount shoe stores that offer the very best of Italian footwear at rock-bottom prices. The styles may not be the hottest or most trending ones, but when you top quality products at really low prices, you don't have any reason to complain. And there's a lot of choice available, so you can be rest assured of finding something just perfect.

Buy Leather Gloves and Jackets

Florence is responsible for creating some of the hottest leather products in the world. As mentioned earlier, San Lorenzo Market is the place for all your leather shopping.

**** PREVIEW OTHER BOOKS BY THIS AUTHOR****

"ROME FOR WOMEN: THE ULTIMATE TRAVEL GUIDE FOR WOMEN" by Erica Stewart

[Excerpt from the first 2 Chapters – for complete book, please purchase on Amazon.com]

Chapter 1: What to Know Before You Go

The urge to be spontaneous, book a cheap flight to Rome and go with the flow may seem romantic and enticing at first thought. Yet ask anyone who's actually tried that and they're likely to bring you back down to earth. Romantic spontaneity is one thing, yet visiting this sprawling metropolis of 2.5 million inhabitants and over 4 million tourists a year, with nothing more than a wing and a prayer – even if that prayer is uttered in the Vatican City - will likely leave you exhausted, frustrated and with not much time on your hands. We're not saying a trip to Rome needs to be approached with German-style military precision, yet it pays to know a little of what to expect, what to avoid and what to keep in mind.

So here's our ultimate list of all we think you should know...before you go.

You can't do it, see it and eat it all

Try as you may, you'll NEVER be able to 'do' Rome in a single visit, so the sooner you accept this fact the better your planning will go. Everything about a visit here is about prioritizing, whether it be attractions, restaurants, dishes or shopping strips. As the saying goes 'Rome was not built in a day' and only the delusional could ever believe they could see it all over a long weekend. Moreover, do you know why so many people are hopelessly in love with the Eternal City? Because they know they can visit once a year, for two decades, and *still* find plenty to see and do. There's a very good reason for that. Rome will offer you 1001 reasons to come back, time and time again. Let her work her magic on you as well.

Which brings us to our next point...

When in Rome, do as the Romans do. Prioritize!

A vacation in Rome may well be a once-in-a-lifetime luxury for many yet even if there is no chance in sight of visiting a second time, you'll still need to prioritize your most fervent wishes in order of preference. Is there a church, an ancient site or a restaurant you've been dying to visit for years? Then put THAT at the top of your list and head forth every day with your list in your pocket. Yes, we know, it's not awfully adventurous to tick items off lists, but if you don't want to head home with more regrets than unforgettable moments, you'd do well to compile a list of your must-dos. Crossing the Mongolian steppe for two weeks on camelback is an adventure; spending your days in Rome walking around like a headless hen because you can't decide what to do first, is just a woeful waste of a golden opportunity. This city is immense, spread out and home to more monuments, museums and landmarks than most other countries. Do yourself a favour: prioritize.

Rome is not nearly as dangerous as it's made out to be. But...

As far as large capital cities are concerned, Rome is no more dangerous than London, New York or Paris, yet also suffers from its fair bout of pickpockets, traps and scams of which you should be aware. By and large, you should be at your most vigilant when in heavily touristy areas and anywhere around the Termini Train Station after sunset. All major transport hubs the world over are quite seedy, but Rome's can be particularly unsavoury, so do have your wits about you. Consolation remains in the fact that overpricing and petty theft is part of life in any major city and at least here it is not only aimed at tourists. Romans get scammed and pick-pocketed just as often as visitors and keep in mind that they spend much less time in the city's touristy areas. Don't pack your most precious jewellery or handbag and don't walk around with your flashy DLR camera around your neck and hundreds of Euros bulging out of your purse and you'll be much less likely to stand out.

You'll be doing a lot of walking. A LOT of walking.

Rome is not Venice. And, in this particular case, it is not Florence either. Rome is an extremely modern, effervescent city which has been spreading its wings far and wide among its priceless ruins for thousands of years. Unfortunately, when Roman Emperors erected their temples, churches, columns and amphitheatres, they had very little regards for what that would mean to tourists a millennia or two later. All of the city's major (and minor) landmarks and highlights are spread out far and wide and across seven vertiginous hills. Considering the rather pesky public transport system (more on this later) to make the best of your visit you're going to have to do a lot of walking, most of which will be uphill. This is one aspect of a Roman visit which many first-timers fail to realize. Pack comfy shoes and leave those sexy heels for a city which is flat and boasts no cobblestone alleyways.

Skip the Metro and get acquainted with the public buses

Many visitors to Rome are understandably petrified of hopping on local buses and we really can't blame them. They are often overcrowded, hardly ever run on time (does anything, in Italy?) and the sheer number of bus numbers and routes to memorize are headache-inducing. Getting familiar with a few bus routes and timetables can be a lot of effort for just a few days' visit BUT if you manage to do just that, your rewards will be tremendous. Due to the number of underground crypts in Rome's most historic core (which is extensive enough as it is), the city's underground Metro steers so far from any point of interest as to make it almost completely useless to tourists. Instead, its buses which ply the routes across the centre. Hopping on them will save you infinite time and leg-ache. One uphill walk saved a day can go a long way in ensuring you don't burn out within just 48 hours of arriving. So channel your inner Roman and learn to love the buses. Pick up a detailed bus timetable from newspaper stands and tobacconists (*tabaccaio* – where you can also purchase bus tickets) and grill your hotel/hostel staff as to all the bus routes to and from your chosen accommodation. Do note that although there are numerous bus passes (for 48 hours or weekly) offered, you are likely never to need them. Single bus tickets cost just €1.50 and are valid for 75 minutes, meaning you can hop on and off different buses at will for 75 minutes after you initially validate your ticket. At most, you will probably only need two tickets a day; considering daily tickets start at €6 they are really not worth the expense. *NB. Bus #64 which plies the tourist route is known locally as the 'pick-pocket express' so avoiding it altogether would be a wise move.*

Pre-planning is ideal

In today's technologically savvy times, there's a bunch of research you can do online before you even arrive, saving you loads of precious vacation time. Download a detailed map of Rome, make sure to note not just distances but walking times (you won't find many maps which denote hills etc) and get acquainted with the bus travel calculator on Google Maps. Surprisingly, this is a lot more efficient than trying to navigate your way through the official ATAC online website. Remember to never rely on travel times as Rome's at-times congested traffic is the only thing which will determine that.

Steer clear of taxis

Rated among the most unscrupulous in all of Europe, taxi drivers in Rome have the uncanny skill of taking the 'Every road leads to Rome' credo to frustratingly new highs. The longest possible driving point between A and B? Yes, they will find it and they will charge you through the nose for it. Best bet? Avoid them (almost) at all costs, especially for getting to and from Fiumicino airport.

Pick the right time to visit

The months of June, July and August are tourist high-season in Rome yet note that this is simply a reflection of European summer school holiday times. The very best months to visit the Italian capital, in fact, are either immediately before or immediately after the summer. April and May, together with September and October are simply splendid and ideal months to visit a city which necessitates so much walking and sightseeing. The scorching summer heat has either not yet arrived or already dissipated, and crowds (although still ever present) will be greatly diminished. Other very popular times (which should be avoided by those on tight budgets and with an aversion to crowds) are Christmas time and Easter Week. Only those who are gluttons for punishment should plan to visit the Vatican City – or any other major landmark - on a Sunday.

Be cunning about WHERE you choose to stay

Rome is both compact and spread out depending on your point of view and affinity for long walks. Walking, by the way, is an incredibly enjoyable activity here as every corner and nook of this glorious city hides ancient treasures and priceless relics. It's fair to assume that you don't want to be too far from the action, but this should not mean that your hotel need be right outside the gates of the Colosseum, far from it. The most interesting hoods to stay in are actually *Trastevere*, the latest *rione* to be gentrified and brimming with cool little cafes' and charming boutiques (not to mention THE best Sunday flea-market in town) and *San Lorenzo*, which is abuzz with young students from the nearby university, and where you'll find the best value-for-money accommodation, dining and drinking options. These areas are particularly ideal for those who want a bit of nightlife right outside their front door. The cheapest area of all is near the Termini Station, but given its insalubrious reputation it is not recommended for ladies travelling alone. The areas around *Piazza Navona* and *Piazza di Spagna* are some of the most popular so tend to be pricier, yet for sheer convenience and elegant ambience they simply can't be beaten.

Load up on fresh, free drinking water

It's all very well to spend weeks on end waiting for that airline ticket to drop by 20 bucks, or begging that hotel manager to include a meagre breakfast with your room rate at no extra charge. But, invariably, you are going to be dropping hundreds and more on expenses you'd probably never envisaged. Drinking water would have to be one of the most overpriced 'luxury' in Rome's tourist centre, due local traders banking on the fact that tourists will avoid the very potable drinking fountains found everywhere in Rome. Don't! The city's *fontanelle* (drinking fountains) have been supplying local inhabitants for thousands of years through ancient Roman aqueducts. Unless you see a sign which says 'non potabile' then go ahead and fill your water bottle with what is, in our humble opinion, the freshest and tastiest drinking water in town.

Need more invaluable insider's info?

Here you go!

Learn (even a little) of the local lingo

It really pays to learn a few Italian phrases before visiting Rome. Italians are not renowned for their command of the English language and, to be brutally honest, many get stroppy if they feel like they should learn a foreign language for the good of tourists. However, you'll be astonished to discover just how friendly and helpful locals can be, the moment you make even the itziest of efforts to communicate in the local lingo. Start every conversation with a *'Buongiorno, come sta?'* (Hello, how are you?) and don't forget to throw in a few *'per favore'* (please) and *'grazie mille'* (thanks a lot) in there for good measure. Before long, you'll find local Romani to be very accommodating indeed. Along with your linguistic education, may as well add the word *'sciopero'* to your vocabulary. This means 'strike' in Italian, it occurs rather too often and usually involves buses, trains and planes.

Opening/Closing times are – more often than not – purely hypothetical

You've finally sussed out an ideal leather shoes outlet store that you absolutely must visit, even if it means hopping on three different buses and spending four hours of your precious day just getting there. You've checked their site online, know it is open and will just get going, right? Wrong! Before you go to any kind of major effort to visit a place/shop/museum/restaurant do make sure that it is, in fact, open. There are some very valid reasons why Swiss are renowned for their punctuality and the Italians not so much! Although *most* major attractions do try their best to operate within their set times, many independent businesses do not, so unless you want to waste your time and cause yourself unnecessary aggravation, source out a phone number and ask a local (be it your new friend at your local café or hotel concierge) to call ahead and confirm.

Plan on getting lost

Well, it's bound to happen sooner or later and although getting hopelessly lost in Rome can be part of the fun, it can also be part of the stress. Always carry a map of Rome with you and the name and address of your accommodation. When asking for directions, do note that Italians are reputedly bad at giving them (this remains a mystery to so many) so don't rely on just one piece of advice. Gather three and go with the majority.

Fight the urge to rent a scooter or – heaven forbid – a car

No matter how many times you've seen La Dolce Vita, do not – and we repeat do not- be tempted to rent a scooter or a car when in Rome. Driving in and around this city necessitates nerves of steel, knowledge of at least half a dozen obscene Italian hand gestures and a very deep religious belief in Padre Pio. Unless you were born in Italy, in which case all of the above-mentioned traits are embedded into your DNA...Do.Not.Drive.

Ditch the guidebook after two days

Visiting Rome and avoiding the Colosseum, Roman Forum or the Vatican would be an absolute travesty and by all means we would never suggest you do that. However, after you have a few of the main sites covered, do put your book away and let your eyes do the guiding. Some of the most magnificent churches are ones which are never mentioned in guide books, including this one! In Rome, even the most inconspicuous little church can hide a Michelangelo and utterly mesmerizing crypts, so walk into every single church, villa, garden or ruin site you come by and you'll be surprised at the treasures you can find.

Skip the tourist foodie traps

Just because Italy and Rome, in particular, is renowned as a foodie haven it does not mean that every meal in every restaurant is going to leave your taste buds jumping for joy. Quite the opposite is true. By and large, it's worth remembering that no restaurant worth its weight in gnocchi will ever employ waiters to stand outside and try to lure diners in, so if you come across one of these near popular piazzas, you'd do well to keep on walking. Generally speaking, the best food in Rome is served in small, family-run places usually hidden in side alleyways with nay a single white table cloth or waiter uniform in sight. Moreover, every Roman resident thinks he or she knows the very bestest little joint in town, so don't be afraid to ask recommendations from everyone you come across who (obviously) speaks a little

English. In a city like Rome, personal recommendations are still the most tried and trusted method of sourcing out the most authentic places. Also worth noting that just because a restaurant is not rated on TripAdvisor, it does not mean it serves bad food. Perhaps, quite the opposite is true. If you come across a lovely looking *trattoria*, full of famished locals beaming happily at a plate of *amatriciana*, then don't be afraid to step right in. But do check prices before you order!

Don't be a tourist!

Yes, you ARE a tourist, but this does not mean you should break the gastronomic cardinal sins of your host country. There's no point going to all sorts of efforts to learn a bit of the lingo and look the part, when you order a *cappuccino* at 3 pm or ask for parmesan cheese for your *marinara*. Mamma mia! Italy is very strict on its food etiquette so know that cappuccino is never ordered past 11 am and never, under any circumstances, should you sprinkle parmesan on any seafood dish. There are a few countries all over the world which boast very strong cuisine cultures, Italy being one of them. Bar what is offered at the table (freshly cracked pepper at most) do not alter a dish with any condiment, lest you risk offending the chef.

Be a Tourist!

No matter what anyone says, head to Rome and skip the Colosseum and you shall be kicking yourself 'till all eternity. The Vatican, Pantheon, Colosseum and Roman Forum are the Holy Trinity(+one!) of Roman sightseeing and an absolute must. An insanely crowded, frustrating must but a must nonetheless. We recommend you visit first thing in the morning and although you can certainly combine the Colosseum and the Forum in one day, the Vatican should really be the highlight on a separate day. Once you have these under your belt, you'll feel free and happy to experience every other treasure this city has to offer.

Skip the line at the Vatican

With most attractions in Rome, it's not worth paying more for a pre-purchased ticket online, yet this is an absolute must for the Vatican City. This is a separate and independent country, so a visit here is not included in any kind of tourist pass in Rome. Pre-purchase your ticket directly from the Vatican Museums Online Ticket Office and skip those heat stroke inducing queues. You will pay about €5 extra, but the privilege of skipping the line is worth every single cent. Don't worry if you arrive later than your predetermined 'visiting time', the Vatican City is not much of a stickler for punctuality either. Your ticket will include entry into the Vatican Museums and the Sistine Chapel, but St Peter's Basilica can only be visited on a tour, so make sure to book that as well. Do note the Vatican has a strict, modest dress code so make sure your shoulders are covered and your skirt/pants end below the knees.

[Excerpt from the first 2 Chapters – for complete book, please purchase on Amazon.com]

Made in the USA
San Bernardino, CA
08 January 2018